Blue Mystery
The Story of the
Hope Diamond

SUSANNE STEINEM PATCH

Blue Mystery
The Story of the
Hope Diamond

SMITHSONIAN INSTITUTION PRESS   WASHINGTON, D.C.   1976

Copyright © 1976 by Susanne Steinem Patch
Smithsonian Institution Press number 6107

Library of Congress Cataloging in Publication Data
Patch, Susanne Steinem.
  Blue mystery: the story of the Hope diamond.
  Bibliography: p.
  1. Hope (Diamond) I. Title.
TS753.P37   736'.23   75-619404
ISBN 0-87474-165-3

Designed by
Natalie Bigelow
Printed in the United States by
Garamond Pridemark Press

Photographic Credits
N. W. Ayer & Son, pp. 34, 35
Diane Beattie, p. 25
Lee Boltin, cover and frontispiece
Du Pont Company, pp. 38, 58
M. Cedric Gleason, p. 21
Harris and Ewing, p. 33
Hessler, p. 33
By courtesy of Lombard Jewelers, Geneva, p. 22
National Museums, Paris, pp. 47, 49
Smithsonian Institution, pp. 31, 36
Washington Star-News, pp. 63, 64.

*Frontispiece: The Hope diamond in its present setting,
the one in which it was given to the Smithsonian
Institution. (Actual size.)*

Contents

To my husband

Foreword

We at the Smithsonian Institution have finally learned to live with the Hope diamond. It has taken a long time! Since it first arrived in 1958 as a gift of Harry Winston, Inc., this infamous diamond has been the Institution's major public attraction and magnet to millions of our visitors. It has been a show stealer, a security problem, a correspondence generator, and an object of wonderment even for the most experienced gemologists and gem connoisseurs.

The National Museum of Natural History, which houses the Hall of Gems, has a visitor load somewhere between three and four million persons each year. Most of the visitors go through the Hall of Gems to get a glimpse of this glittering blue treasure. They come in such numbers that, in the peak of the tourist season, the crowds far exceed the capacity of the room in which the diamond is kept.

What do they see? Certainly, they don't see just a diamond. This is a very special diamond and perhaps is the best known gem in the world. It is difficult to see it only as a diamond when the world's literature is full of the legend of its curse. Above all, it is the mysteriously cursed diamond which is popularly held responsible for all sorts of misfortunes, real or imagined. Shortly after the Hope diamond went on public exhibit, letters began to arrive in the Smithsonian's voluminous daily mail, blaming the gem for all misfortunes from presidential assassination to the atom bomb to stock market reverses, war, and economic recession. Such is the power of the myth that has been built around this diamond, which needs none of it to be famous. It is a beautiful, rare, and extraordinarily fine and interesting gem in its own right, a king among diamonds.

Some visitors are not sure they are looking at a real diamond. They suspect instead that it is a clever imitation. No amount of assurance will convince them that the Hope diamond and all of its dazzling neighbors in the Hall of Gems are real. Some are puzzled at finding the gems in a room immediately adjacent to the Museum's excellent display of minerals, forgetting that gems are nothing more than unusually fine and valuable bits of minerals. Nevertheless, almost all visitors leave with the sense of having seen something truly important in the coldly winking, blue diamond resting in its private show vault.

The shape into which the stone has been cut is not as good as it might be, but this cannot detract from the fact that it is flawless, has a very rare color, and, at 45½ carats, is a large diamond. Since there is no other diamond like it, frequent questions about its value are meaningless. It is priceless! The Hope diamond will never be available to the gem market again but it would surely bring several millions of dollars if offered for sale. This means that the National Museum of Natural History must face up to a difficult security responsibility. The responsibility is further complicated because there are many millions of dollars worth of other gems clustered in other exhibits in the Hall of Gems. Of course, all of this treasure is carefully guarded day and night by Smithsonian guards, plainclothes detectives, K-9 patrols, sophisticated electronic devices of various sorts, special kinds of glass for the show cases, and special viewing vaults for the more important gems. This would be necessary even if the Hope diamond had no fascinating legend to embellish its beauty.

And what about the legendary curse of the Hope diamond? How does the Smithsonian view it? My own personal attitude is as official as any, i.e., *the curse does not exist*. It is a carefully nurtured fairy tale based on just enough fact to make it believable. With a little distortion of the true facts, and a careful selection of those incidents which are pertinent to it, the legend has been embellished and perpetuated. Susanne Patch, the author of this book, has done an excellent and careful job of searching out every scrap of the history of this fabulous gem. She presents here all the information known to the Smithsonian about the Hope diamond and, in a most scientific manner, discusses it. On the following pages she shares her discoveries with us in such a way that, with or without the legendary curse, every reader will acquire a new respect for this "Blue Mystery."

PAUL E. DESAUTELS
Curator in charge, National
Collection of Gems

Preface

Minerals, particularly those rare and beautiful enough to be gems, have been my lifelong interest. When I was director of an educational diamond exhibit I became familiar with the stories of all the famous diamonds and found that of the Hope most fascinating because of the mystery surrounding its origin. A desire to dispel that mystery started me on my research, and the many inconsistencies in the diamond's history spurred me on. How, for example, could one of its owners, the actress May Yohe, be pictured in a newspaper clipping supposedly wearing the Hope diamond in the mounting that was made for its subsequent owner, Evalyn Walsh McLean?

An exciting moment in my research came when, through great good luck, I uncovered two original sketches of the Hope diamond made in 1812. These drawings document the diamond's existence in its present form eighteen years earlier than the 1830 date usually given for its first appearance.

Just as this book was going to press, museum authorities permitted the Hope diamond to be removed from its mounting and weighed. It was found that the diamond weighs 45.52 carats (in modern metric carats). This is discussed further on page 62. The most exciting moment of all for me occurred when, placing the Hope diamond upside down on a slip of white paper, I—like the lapidary in 1812—"traced [it] round the diamond with a pencil" and discovered that the outline I had drawn, complete with one flattened side, was identical to the earlier drawing.

Many questions still remain unanswered; and perhaps the Hope diamond, like the complex and powerful people who have been driven to possess it, can never be completely known. But if any reader has additional information to contribute about the tantalizing gaps in this diamond's history, please write to me in care of the Smithsonian Institution Press, Washington, D.C. 20560.

Susanne Steinem Patch

Acknowledgments

A number of people have been of assistance in the preparation of this book. From the Smithsonian Institution, I wish to thank Dr. George S. Switzer, former Curator of the Department of Mineral Sciences. We first discussed the Hope diamond about fifteen years ago and he has always responded cordially to requests for assistance. My thanks go especially to Paul Desautels, Curator of the Division of Mineralogy. Without his encouragement the present book would not have been written. The editing was in the capable hands of Hope Pantell, a most appropriately named editor of the Smithsonian Institution Press. Jack Marquardt and Carolyn Hahn of the Smithsonian Libraries searched out many valuable resource materials. From the United States Geological Survey, I am grateful to George H. Goodwin, Jr., Chief Librarian, and Hartley K. Phinney, Chief, Reference and Circulation, for their cooperation.

I would also like to thank the following people who were kind enough to provide information used in this book: Diane Beattie, cousin of May Yohe; Dorothy Dignam, formerly of N.W. Ayer & Son; J. Timberlake Gibson, author; M. Cedric Gleason, collector of rare gem books; Dr. F. H. M. Grapperhaus, president-director of Bank Mees and Hope N.V. Amsterdam (successor to Hope & Co.); Nancy Harris of the Smithsonian; Katherine Rockwell Huse, former reporter for the Manchester (New Hampshire) *Union;* Florence McDermott of N.W. Ayer & Son; His Grace, the Duke of Newcastle, son of Lord Francis Hope; Charles Schwartz of Charles Schwartz & Son, jewelers; Ruth N. Steinem for help in locating theatrical archives; Matilda Tyler for material about Marie Antoinette; and Mary Winters for help with French translations.

My thanks go as well to Ann Wallington, who typed the manuscript; to my sister, Gloria Steinem, for her helpful comments; to my daughter, Susan, for assistance with corrections; to my other children for their forbearance; and to my husband, Robert, who helped in many ways.

What Is Known about the Hope Diamond

A tiny fragment of midnight sky, fallen to earth and still aglow with star gleam.—from a 1947 report in the *Washington Post*

An ominous unearthly stone with millions of sardonic winks.—Jules Jusserand, former French ambassador to the United States, about 1915

These are just two of the descriptions inspired by the Hope diamond, one of the world's most beautiful gems, during its long and fabulous passage from one proud possessor to another.

Now, the Hope diamond has come to rest in a specially constructed glass-fronted vault in the Hall of Gems at the Smithsonian's National Museum of Natural History. Its previous owner, the noted New York jeweler Harry Winston, gave the Hope to the Smithsonian in 1958, and an estimated fifty million people have been able to witness its unique beauty since then.

The intimate history of the Hope lives on, even inside the vault. Surrounded by sixteen diamonds and suspended from a necklace containing forty-six more diamonds, all set in platinum, the Hope is a glittering personal adornment. If visitors look closely, they will see a small platinum hook at the bottom of the pendant. It was put there in 1911 at the request of the legendary Evalyn Walsh McLean, the last private owner of the Hope, so that she could suspend yet another famous diamond below the huge blue brilliant: a 94⅘-carat, pear-shaped white diamond known as the Star of the East.

The very odd deep blue of the Hope diamond—once poetically described as "indignant indigo"—is one of the rarest of diamond colors; combined with an outstanding size of slightly more than 45½ carats, it makes this diamond unique. Yet many people who come to see the Hope are surprised to discover that it is blue. What brings them, many from great distances, to see it is revealed by their questions, "Does it really bring bad luck?" "Is it true that everyone who owned it died?" They are obviously responding to the persistent and much publicized legend that the Hope diamond affects tragically the lives of those who own or wear it.

The legend begins with the story that more than 300 years ago the diamond was stolen from the eye or forehead of an idol in India worshipped by the followers of Rama Sita. The theft is supposed to have caused the god to place a curse not only upon the robber but also upon all subsequent owners of the diamond. Though the diamond was *not* stolen from the eye or forehead of an idol, as this account will explain, the idea of a curse, a haunting aura of bad luck, still follows the Hope—and there are some events that support the fear.

Perhaps it is only that believing in bad luck makes the believer more vulnerable. Perhaps, in searching for the cause of personal troubles, each owner of the diamond blamed the legend of the Hope, and thus increased it. Whatever the reason, this blue and brilliant object continues to excite both fascination and fear, even safely enclosed in its sealed vault.

Tracing the history of the Hope diamond, including its speculative link to the famous French blue diamond, and looking at the lives of its owners, may help to explain the development of the legend.

EARLY HISTORY

It is possible to follow the history of even major gemstones only if they are so remarkable that some note has often been made of their appearance. It is the extraordinary dark blue color of this large stone that has led historians to speculate that it may have been cut from the French blue diamond stolen in 1792 from the French crown jewels.

Its first appearance as recorded in most histories, however, occurred in 1830 when Henry Philip Hope, the London banker whose name is still attached to the gem, purchased it from Daniel Eliason, a London diamond merchant. The price, a huge sum for its day, was £18,000 (about $90,000).

Large diamonds are uncommon and customarily come on the market with a pedigree of some sort; the Hope diamond did not. It "came to light without a history, without any account being rendered as to whence it came and what had been its travels and fortunes."[1] Because of this, most histories of the diamond begin in 1830. It is, however, possible to begin its story a little earlier.

In the 1823 edition of his book *A Treatise on Diamonds and Precious Stones*, John Mawe described a superlatively fine blue diamond weighing 44 carats and valued at £30,000. "This unrivaled gem is of a deep sapphire blue, and from its rarity and color might have been estimated at a higher sum." Mawe's book has an illustration showing "Peculiar Diamonds," in which figures 4 and 5 are top and side views of the diamond he describes—and it clearly has the same proportions and shape as the Hope. He also mentioned that this stone had been in the hands of "Mr. Eliason, an eminent Diamond merchant." This information and the publication date of the book prove that the blue diamond in its present shape was known in London prior to 1823. Mawe recorded in 1823 the rumor that Eliason had sold the diamond to "our most gracious sovereign" (George IV). Since Hope purchased the diamond from Eliason in 1830, however, this must have been untrue.

The first edition of Mawe's book, printed in 1813, mentions in a footnote "a superlatively fine blue diamond, of above 44 carats, in the possession of an individual in London." While not conclusive in itself, when this is read in conjunction with the later edition, it is clear that it is the Hope which is being described.

There is other evidence which places a 44-carat blue diamond in England at least as early as 1812. George Frederick Kunz, a distinguished American gemologist, told of finding two detailed sketches of the Hope diamond made by a Soho lapidary in 1812. As he explained in an article in the *Saturday Evening Post* of January 21, 1928, Kunz discovered the sketches in an old book on the jeweler's art by Pouget that he found one day while browsing in Quaritch's book shop in London.

Kunz, who died in 1932, left his professional library to the United States Geological Survey. That collection contains two copies of the Pouget book, one of which has been

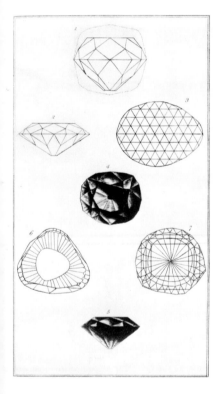

"Peculiar Diamonds," illustration from an 1823 book by John Mawe. Numbers 4 and 5 show the top and side views of the blue diamond owned by diamond merchant Daniel Eliason, which was later purchased by Henry Philip Hope.

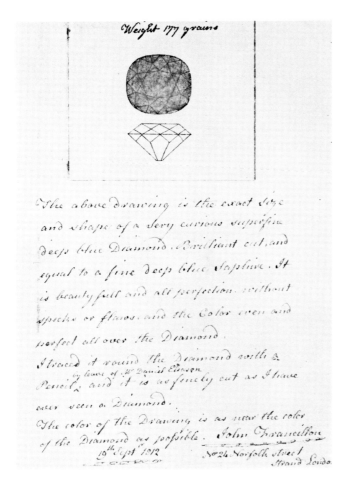

John Françillon's statement, with top and side views of the diamond.

rebound. Apparently Kunz himself had the second book rebound, and included the sketches referred to above. In this way the original drawings and notations have been preserved. The first drawing consists of a pencil outline of the diamond with the notation "the original tracing of the brilliant," plus the original notes. The second shows the top and side views of the diamond in detail with the caption "weight 177 grains" and a formal statement as follows:

> The above drawing is the exact size and shape of a very curious superfine deep blue Diamond. Brilliant cut, and equal to a fine deep blue Sapphire. It is beauty full and all perfection without specks or flaws, and the Color even and perfect all over the Diamond.
> I traced it round the diamond with a Pencil by leave of Mr. Daniel Eliason and it is as finely cut as I have ever seen a Diamond.
> The color of the Drawing is as near the color of the Diamond as possible.

dated: 19th Septer 1812

John Françillon
No 26 Norfolk Street
Strand. London

To anyone familiar with the Hope diamond, it is immediately apparent, because of its one flattened side, that the outline is that of the Hope. A check with the Smithsonian confirmed that the dimensions of the sketch are identical with those of the Hope. That it was possible to draw around the diamond shows that in 1812 the diamond was unset.

19

THE HOPE FAMILY   While no one knows from whom Daniel Eliason purchased the Hope diamond, quite a bit is known about Henry Philip Hope, the man to whom he sold it.

Henry Philip Hope was a descendant of the Amsterdam Hopes, a family of merchant bankers. Their firm, Hope & Co., was formed in 1762 and, between 1770 and 1815, was the most renowned in Europe. The firm made loans to many countries, among them Sweden, Russia, Spain, and Portugal. Between 1788 and 1793 Hope & Co. issued loans to Russia of approximately $21,400,000. Henry Hope, uncle of Henry Philip Hope, was so esteemed by Catherine the Great that she offered to ennoble him (an honor he declined) and gave him a picture of herself. That portrait now hangs in "Hillwood," the former Washington residence of the late Marjorie Merriweather Post, which she bequeathed to the Smithsonian Institution.

A little known fact, important in American history, is that Hope & Co., together with the London house of Baring, financed the Louisiana Purchase. (The youthful United States established a good credit record because it was prompt in making payments on its loans.)

By 1813 the last active partner in Hope & Co. had died and the heirs, of whom Henry Philip Hope was one, sold out to the Baring firm.

Henry Philip Hope has been described as ". . . very wealthy, but a man of simple habits and munificent in his charities."[2] Simple habits or not, collecting art, diamonds, and other precious stones was his hobby. The Dutch and Flemish paintings that he bought he added to a collection begun earlier by his eldest brother.

Hope asked Bram Hertz, himself a collector, to make a catalog of Hope's gem collection, which was valued at £150,000. Published in August 1839, the catalog was in two parts: the first, containing descriptions of the jewels, and the second, showing line drawings of them. The jewels were kept in a large mahogany case with sixteen drawers, each covered with glass and numbered. The descriptive ticket which accompanied each gem was made of ivory and had the catalog number of the gem and its carat weight engraved on it. It is apparent from the catalog that Hope had a special interest in unusual gems.

Hope, who liked "fancy" (colored) diamonds, had forty-one cut diamonds of unusual hues in addition to other colored diamonds still in their natural form. In the catalog the Hope diamond is described as being mounted as a medallion (brooch) with a border *en arabesque* of small rose diamonds, surrounded by twenty brilliant cut diamonds of equal size, shape, and cutting, and of the finest water and averaging four grains each. (The grain is a unit of weight most commonly used for pearls, but, especially in earlier times, it was sometimes used for diamonds. Since a grain is equal to fifty milligrams or one-quarter of a carat, the twenty brilliants would have averaged one carat each.) In color the Hope diamond is described in the catalog as a fine deep sapphire blue.

Among the pearls listed is the famous Hope pearl, weighing 1,800 grains, or more than three ounces. Of an irregular pear shape, this pearl is greenish bronze in color at the large end, gradually becoming a fine white at the smaller end. It is two inches long and four and one-half inches in circumference at its broadest point, and is topped

A

CATALOGUE

OF THE

COLLECTION

OF

PEARLS AND PRECIOUS STONES

FORMED

BY HENRY PHILIP HOPE, ESQ.

SYSTEMATICALLY ARRANGED AND DESCRIBED

BY B. HERTZ.

LONDON:

PRINTED BY WILLIAM CLOWES AND SONS, STAMFORD STREET.

August. 1839.

POLISHED DIAMONDS.

No. 1*. A most magnificent and rare brilliant, of a deep sapphire blue, of the greatest purity, and most beautifully cut; it is of true proportions, not too thick, nor too spread. This matchless gem combines the beautiful colour of the sapphire with the prismatic fire and brilliancy of the diamond, and, on account of its extraordinary colour, great size, and other fine qualities, it certainly may be called unique; as we may presume that there exists no cabinet, nor any collection of crown jewels in the world, which can boast of the possession of so curious and fine a gem as the one we are now describing; and we expect to be borne out in our opinion by our readers, since there are extant historical records and treatises on the precious gems, which give us descriptions of all the extraordinary diamonds in the possession of all the crowned heads of Europe, as well as of the princes of Eastern countries. But in vain do we search for any record of a gem which can, in point of curiosity, beauty, and perfection, be compared with this blue brilliant.

Diamonds are found of almost every colour, which is proved by the great variety of coloured diamonds in this collection; but the blue colour is the most rare and most valuable, since there has very seldom been found a diamond of any size of a fine deep sapphire blue, those which are termed blue diamonds being generally of a very light or of a steel-blue colour: it would, therefore, be a difficult task to form a just estimate of the value of this unrivalled gem, there being no precedent, the value cannot be established by comparison. The price which was once asked for this diamond was 30,000l., but we must confess, for the above-stated reasons, that it might have been estimated even at a higher sum. To convey to the reader by a description a just conception of the beauty and splendour of this unique production of nature would be a vain attempt.

This beautiful gem is most tastefully mounted as a medallion, with a border *en arabesque* of small rose diamonds, surrounded by 20 brilliants of equal size, shape, and cutting, and of the finest water, and averaging four grains each. Its weight is 177 grains.

This gem, particularly on account of its mounting, could not be placed in the drawer with the diamonds, but is kept in Drawer 16, together with the other extraordinary specimens of this collection.—Vide plate 5.

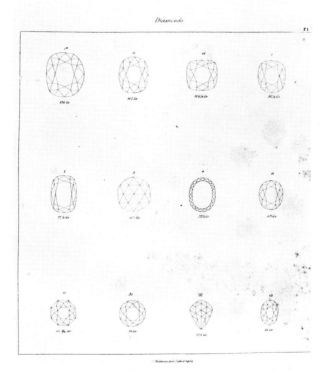

The 1839 catalog of Henry Philip Hope's gem collection describes the Hope diamond and shows a line drawing, upper left-hand corner, of it.

The Hope pearl, one of the world's largest, was formerly in the collection of Henry Philip Hope, along with the Hope diamond. The pearl is topped with a red enameled gold crown set with diamonds, rubies, emeralds, and sapphires. Because the style of the crown is French, some believe it to have once been in the French crown jewels.

22

by an arched crown of red enameled gold set with diamonds, rubies, and emeralds. Because this crown is in the French style, some writers believe that the gem may once have been part of the French crown jewels. The Hope pearl, after having dropped from sight for a number of years, was privately offered for sale in 1974 for $200,000.

Henry Philip Hope was one of three brothers. Not much is known of Adrian Elias, the middle one. The eldest brother, Thomas Hope, has been described as an artist and virtuoso, a great collector of ancient sculptures, vases, Italian paintings, and other works of art. His collections were housed in two residences, one on Duchess Street near Cavendish Square, London, and the other a mansion at Deepdene in Surrey. He wrote a number of books which were highly praised, including some on interior design, modern costumes, and architecture. His best known work was a romance entitled *Anastasius or Memoirs of a Greek written at the close of the Eighteenth Century.* The poet Byron said that he "wept bitterly on reading 'Anastasius' for two reasons—one that he had not written it, and the other that Hope had."[3] Thomas Hope died in 1831, leaving three sons.

Henry Philip Hope had never married and when he died, in 1839, he left large fortunes to each of his three nephews. Henry Thomas Hope (1808-1862), the eldest, who had inherited from his father the family residence in London and the mansion at Deepdene, now also had a large collection of art and the Hope diamond. It is not clear whether the diamond was bequeathed to him or whether he purchased it from his uncle's estate.

Groom of the bedchamber to King George IV and for many years a member of Parliament for the city of Gloucester, Henry Thomas Hope was married and had a daughter, Henrietta Adéla. He displayed the Hope diamond at the Crystal Palace Exhibition of 1851 in London, at which the famous Koh-i-noor diamond was also exhibited. The Koh-i-noor, an Indian diamond whose history goes back to 1304, had been presented to Queen Victoria only the year before. Given by the East India Company to mark the 250th anniversary of its founding, the gem then weighed 186 carats (it would later be recut) and was valued at $700,000.

Hope was only fifty-four when he died, and his widow and daughter were his heirs. Henrietta Adéla had married Henry Pelham Alexander, son of the fifth Duke of Newcastle-under-Lyme, in 1861 and had five children, two sons and three daughters. Since the elder son stood to inherit the title and estates of the Duke of Newcastle, Hope's widow, who had retained the diamond, left in her will of 1876 a life interest in her property to the second son, probably with the proviso that he adopt the name of the Hope family. This he did on April 7, 1887, thus becoming Henry Francis Hope Pelham-Clinton-Hope. Then twenty-one years old, he acquired a life interest in various estates, among them Deepdene in Surrey, plus certain heirlooms, which included the Hope diamond. (If he, Lord Francis Hope, were to die without issue, his elder sister would inherit the life interest. If she died without sons, the second sister would inherit the life interest, and so on through the family.)

Information about Lord Francis Hope must be culled primarily from newspaper accounts and from legal records; the Hope family archives were destroyed in the bombing of London in 1940. His Grace, the present Duke of Newcastle (son of Lord Francis Hope), says he has no direct information about these matters because his mother died when he was only five years old and his father would never discuss the Hope diamond.

From legal records it can be discovered that, even though the Hope estates produced an annual income in excess of $80,000, Lord Francis was in financial difficulties in 1893 at the age of twenty-seven. He petitioned the court for permission to sell the collection of Dutch and Flemish paintings in which his grandmother had left him a life interest, but his brother and three sisters opposed the sale, and the petition was denied. Lord Francis must therefore have been very short of money when he married an American actress, May Yohe, in 1894.

Born Mary Augusta Yohe in 1869, May was the daughter of a seamstress. Her family seems to have belonged to a less affluent branch of a large and well-to-do Pennsylvania clan, possibly descended from William Penn. When she made her debut as a singer in Bethlehem, Pennsylvania, her voice was so impressive that the miners are supposed to have taken up a subscription to pay for her operatic training in Paris. To the horror of her sponsors, she joined a burlesque show in Pittsburgh as a chorus girl when she first returned to the United States. After a few months, however, she made her operatic debut at the Temple Theatre in Philadelphia. In 1887, at eighteen, May was given the lead in an extravaganza called *The Crystal Slipper*, which was a great success. Nevertheless, after several weeks, "Madcap May Yohe," as she was known, ran off to Buffalo with Ely B. Shaw, the son of a wealthy Chicagoan. She soon returned to the show, however, when it developed that Shaw was already married.

The Crystal Slipper toured America for several seasons. May said in later years that she met Lord Francis Hope in New York just before she left for England to star in the musical *Christopher Columbus*, in which she sang "Honey, Mah Honey" and "What Can a Poor Girl Do," winning acclaim from the London critics. She had a deep contralto voice and, in what seems an unflattering reference but was intended to be admiring, she was called the "girl with the fog-horn voice."

Lord Francis Hope and May were secretly married in Hempstead, England, on November 27, 1894. May Yohe said they had lived together for five or six months before they were married. She also said, however, that she was married at eighteen, while simple arithmetic makes it twenty-five. For this "eighteenth birthday," according to May, Hope gave her "a string of gorgeous pear-shaped pearls," for which he paid $350,000 to a famous jeweler, who had scoured Europe for the perfectly matched gems.[4] It is difficult to see, if he needed money in 1893, how he could have bought a $350,000 necklace in 1894, but perhaps he did (although a perfectly matched string of *all* pear-shaped pearls is implausible). In any case, in 1895 Lord Francis became bankrupt. At that time his life interest in the estates was vested in trustees who would only pay him the equivalent of ten thousand dollars a year. The residue of the income was to be held in trust until a "sinking fund" or residue fund of £210,000 had accumulated.

Lord Francis's financial difficulties were primarily caused by his gambling. After his

May Yohe, Lady Francis Hope

bankruptcy, May, who was having a great success on the English stage, contributed to their support. Hope obtained his discharge from bankruptcy in 1896. By 1898 he was back in court again to petition for approval of the sale of the Dutch and Flemish paintings. This time, his family's opposition having been withdrawn, the petition was granted and the paintings were sold for £121,550. The income from the sale went into the sinking fund, however, so Lord Francis was no better off than before.

Hope next petitioned the court to approve a conditional contract made in December 1898 with L. M. Lowenstein and Company for the sale of the Hope diamond, which was described as being set in a brooch surrounded by twenty-two brilliants. In an affidavit read on behalf of Lord Francis, Edwin W. Streeter, a jeweler of New Bond Street, estimated the value of the diamond at £18,115. Hope declared that the diamond had not been used for many years and had, since 1894, been deposited at Parr's Bank, Cavendish Square, and it therefore afforded neither pleasure nor utility to himself or his wife. (May is supposed to have worn the Hope diamond only twice, once after she was married in 1894 and once in 1900. She had plenty of other jewelry—much of it gifts from admirers.)

Once again, however, there was opposition from the remainder of the family: Lord Francis Hope's three sisters and his elder brother, the seventh Duke of Newcastle, opposed the sale of the Hope diamond. The application for permission to sell the diamond was heard on May 16, 1899, before a judge who denied the request, in part because there was a big difference between experts on its proper valuation.

Lord Francis appealed the case, and the appeal was heard before two judges on July 14 and 15, 1899. The request was again denied. Each of the judges involved in the original case and the appeal took the opportunity to lecture Lord Francis on his extravagance, and to point out that it was quite obvious that he had brought his difficulties upon himself.

85048

One of the appeal judges, sympathizing with the desire of the rest of the family to retain the diamond, said, ". . . we cannot judicially ignore the fact that this is a very beautiful and at present almost unique diamond of a colour and size not seen in modern times."[5] Hope still had the right to appeal the case to the House of Lords.

In 1900 Lord Francis and Lady May Hope visited the United States. It was on this trip that Lady May met Putnam Bradlee Strong, the son of a former mayor of New York, William L. Strong. May later wrote of Strong, "He was a fascinating man, with a suave gallantry which charmed women. I never have known a woman who, after being thrown in Captain Strong's company for awhile, did not fall in love with him— wife or maid or widow, it was always the same."[6] May was no exception, but Lord Francis must have been blind to the attraction between his wife and his friend for later on, when Hope sued for divorce, he testified that he didn't notice any change in his wife's behavior until March 1901 even though it was only a month later that May left him for good. By April she and Strong, traveling as husband and wife under assumed names, departed for Japan.

That fall, after a long legal fight, Lord Francis finally succeeded in securing permission to dispose of the Hope diamond. It was sold in 1901 by order of a Master in Chancery in London.

The sale of the diamond does not seem to have helped Hope very much. The purchase price would have gone into the trust, of course, so he could receive only the interest as income. On the grounds of his wife's misconduct with Strong, Hope obtained a divorce in March 1902, but in April he was bankrupt again. In various later lists of the tragedies which are supposed to have befallen Lord Francis because he owned the Hope diamond, moreover, one has never been mentioned. The *New York Times*, in its article at the time of the divorce, said Lord Francis ". . . is still suffering from the amputation of his leg. . . ." Other clippings disclose that this was the aftermath of a hunting accident in which Hope accidentally shot himself in the leg.

In spite of newspaper reports that Lord Francis was engaged to marry a cousin, Beatrice Ricketts, as soon as his divorce became final, he did not remarry until 1904. His bride, for whom it was also a second marriage, was an Englishwoman named Olive Muriel Thompson Owen. One more tragedy from this period must be recorded: Hope's second wife, after bearing three children, died in 1912, only eight years after their wedding.

When his elder brother died, childless, in 1928, Lord Francis Hope succeeded him, becoming the eighth Duke of Newcastle at the age of sixty-two. He died at seventy-five and was succeeded by his only son, Henry Edward Hugh, the ninth and present Duke. Except for the early financial difficulties of his father, the Duke would likely have been the present-day owner of the diamond which still bears the name of his ancestors.

Meanwhile, following her separation from Lord Francis, May Yohe had arrived in Japan with Captain Strong. There they rented a house which was once used as a guest house by the Prince of Wales and began giving elaborate parties. Everything went well until May's money started to run out. Since Strong's family disapproved of her they wouldn't help the couple, and Strong began to sell May's jewelry in order to cover their debts. They married when her divorce from Lord Francis became final, but in the following years they were separated and reconciled several times. In the meantime, Strong, without her consent, had sold the remainder of her jewels. The Strongs were divorced in 1910.

Attempting a comeback in 1912, May appeared in a revival of *Little Christopher Columbus*, which opened in London to mixed reviews. Lord Francis had a box seat for opening night and, although May had earlier called him undemonstrative, he is reported to have wept when she appeared. It was for this performance that May first wore a copy of the Hope diamond.

While on a theater engagement in South Africa, May met Captain John Smuts, a cousin of Boer General Jan Smuts. She married him in 1914. When Smuts was forced to retire from the service because of a wound received during the First World War, he and May moved to Singapore. After three years on a rubber plantation there, Smuts became permanently disabled and he and May came to the United States.

The couple spent the summer of 1919 in a house in Quebec Province, Canada, that belonged to May's cousin, Adeline Cummings Parke. Her cousin's daughter, Diane Beattie, then eight years old, spent the summer with them and remembers them as very much in love, with never a cross word spoken.

Economically, the Smutses didn't fare very well, engaging in a series of ill-fated, small-business ventures (chicken farming and ranching, among others). As each one failed, May would return to the stage, where she always seemed to enjoy a fair success, to earn money for the next venture. For all her stage appearances she wore her replica of the blue diamond, which gave rise to false reports that she had taken the real diamond with her when she left Lord Francis Hope. The confusion was increased by the mounting, which was a copy of the one made especially for Mrs. McLean when she purchased the Hope diamond in 1911. In 1923 May was appearing with a jazz band at the Palace Theater in Manchester, New Hampshire. Then in her fifties, May gave an interview to reporter Katherine Rockwell (now Mrs. Robert Huse of Chevy Chase, Maryland). Although May had not worn the Hope diamond for at least twenty-one years, its influence was still apparent as she told of the Smutses' latest venture, the remodeling of a Marlborough, New Hampshire, farmhouse into a tea room to be called the Blue Diamond Inn. The inn burned down, and eventually May worked for the Works Progress Administration (WPA) as a researcher. She died in 1938 at age sixty-nine.

FIRST AMERICAN OWNER

When Lord Francis Hope finally was able to sell the Hope diamond in 1901, the buyer was Simon Frankel of a New York firm of diamond merchants, Joseph Frankel's Sons. Boyd's New York directory for 1900 gives the firm's address as 68 Nassau Street. Simon Frankel actually purchased the diamond in London and returned with it to New York on the North German Lloyd liner *Kronprinz Wilhelm*, which docked on November 26, 1901. During the voyage the diamond had been locked in the vessel's strongbox.

27

Although the price paid for the diamond was rumored to have been $250,000, the value given on the invoice, on which a 10 percent customs duty was paid, was $141,032. Frankel said he had not bought it for a particular customer but for business purposes.

Putting together the information given by W. R. Cattelle and Julius Wodiska in their books, each written within a few years of the event, the Frankel firm sold the Hope diamond in the spring of 1908 to a certain Habib (Habid?) of the rue Laffitte, Paris, proprietor of a collection of rare gems.[7] A little more than a year later, the Hope diamond changed hands again.

A 1909 news story on page 1 of the *New York Times* bears the headline "Hope Diamond Goes Cheap." Datelined Paris, June 24, it says: "The famous Hope diamond went for only $80,000 at the sale of the Habib Collection today. The collector paid $400,000 for it. It was bought today by Louis Aucoc, the leading diamond expert of France, presumably for a customer."

Other sources say a diamond merchant named Rosenau bought it at the Paris auction. Aucoc and Rosenau were both purchasers of record when most of the French crown jewels were sold at auction in 1887. It is possible that the two men bought it in partnership; with so much money involved, an arrangement of this kind would not be uncommon.

There was a rumor at the time that Habib had acted as an agent for Abdul-Hamid, Sultan of Turkey, when he purchased the diamond in 1908 and again when he sold it in 1909. This has never been proved. As reported in the *New York Times*, the Sultan's jewels were sold in December 1911.

The Cartier firm in Paris said it acquired the Hope diamond from Rosenau.[8] It was Pierre Cartier who sold the blue diamond to the woman whose name has become almost synonymous with that of the diamond—Evalyn Walsh McLean.

THE McLEANS

From the time in 1896 when Thomas F. Walsh confided to his ten-year-old, "Daughter, I've struck it rich!" to the day of his death in 1910, Tom Walsh enjoyed his money and used it lavishly, not least on his adored daughter, Evalyn. The Camp Bird gold mine in Colorado was the source of the Walshes' wealth, at one time producing ore worth about $5,000 a day.

The Walshes and their two children, Evalyn and her younger brother, Vinson, moved to Washington, D.C., from Colorado in 1897 and were soon part of Washington society. Only two years later President McKinley appointed Walsh a commissioner to the Paris Exposition. Shortly afterward, Walsh built a mansion at 2020 Massachusetts Avenue that cost $865,000 and contained a magnificent staircase copied from the one on the White Star liner which the Walshes had taken to Paris. Evalyn "swiped crème de menthe from his [her father's] liquor closet, squandered her allowance on ermine tails, and ruined the nerves of a series of hapless governesses."[9]

By age twelve, Evalyn had persuaded her father to provide her with a carriage, a pair of horses, and a coachman so she could drive to school in style. One major tragedy marred those early years. Vinson, twenty months younger than Evalyn, died in an automobile accident in which Evalyn was also injured, leaving her with one leg shorter than the other.

In July 1908 Evalyn Walsh married Edward Beale McLean, son of John R. McLean, owner of two newspapers, the *Cincinnati Enquirer* and the *Washington Post*. The newlyweds were both twenty-two years old. Their fathers gave each of them $100,000 before they left on their European honeymoon but, after having been gone a little less than four months, they ran out of money and wired their fathers for assistance. Walsh sent Evalyn a fresh credit and his love. Ned McLean received a telegram, "Better hurry home January first for *Washington Post* meeting."[10] In her autobiography, Evalyn Walsh McLean said that Ned "never had been allowed so much as I. Indeed, that $100,000 of his that we had blown along with my own $100,000 had been intended by John R. to set us up in life. He was, according to Walsh standards, tight."[11]

Just before they left Europe, Evalyn remembered that she had not yet found the wedding present her father had asked her to select. So she went to Cartier's and explained her predicament. Then, said Evalyn, the salesman "hypnotized me by showing me an ornament that made bright spots before my eyes. (Anyway that's what I told my father later.)"[12] It was a necklace of square links of platinum set with diamonds from which hung three loops of diamonds. Attached to the bottom loop was a pearl of 32¼ grains, the size of a little finger tip; suspended below it was a six-sided emerald weighing 34½ carats, and hanging below that was the Star of the East, a pear-shaped diamond weighing almost 95 carats.

Let Mrs. McLean tell the rest. "With fingers that fumbled from excitement I put that gorgeous piece around my throat. 'Ned,' I said in mock despair, 'it's got me! I'll never get away from the spell of this.'

" 'A shock might break the spell,' said Ned. 'Suppose you ask the price of this magnificence.'

" 'Well,' I said to the man at Cartier's as I put my index fingers in my ears, 'how much?'

"He whispered, 'Six hundred thousand francs, madame.'

" 'You mean a hundred and twenty thousand dollars?'

"He cocked his head to one side so that his nod was made obliquely.

" 'After all,' I said to Ned, 'This is really an investment. Besides this is December fifteenth and I can tell my father it's a double gift, to cover both my wedding and Christmas.'

"So we signed a receipt and Cartier allowed us children to walk out with the Star of the East."[13]

Evalyn Walsh McLean first saw the Hope diamond when she and her husband were visiting Paris in 1910, about six months after the birth of her first child, Vinson, and only a few months after the death of her father. Pierre Cartier brought the diamond to the McLeans' hotel and regaled them with its past history, "or what he freely acknowledged were his beliefs concerning that history."[14] He claimed that Mrs. McLean had told him in an earlier conversation that she had seen one of the members of the Sultan's harem wearing the blue diamond when the McLeans visited Turkey on their honeymoon. Mrs. McLean did not contradict Cartier at that time, but in her autobiography she wrote that she did not, in fact, remember seeing it, although she had seen other jewels that, as she put it, "made my fingers itch." She also wrote "Did the Turkish Sultan, Abdul-Hamid, ever own it? I do not know for sure. Cartier told me his firm acquired it from a man named Rosenau in Paris."[15]

Cartier told her that the diamond was supposed to bring bad luck to anyone who wore it, or even touched it. This was actually an attraction for Mrs. McLean, as Cartier knew it would be, because she had previously told him that she felt bad-luck objects were lucky for her. The mounting didn't appeal to her, however, and she dismissed the diamond without ever finding out the price.

Several months later, when the McLeans were home again in Washington, they received a note from Cartier's saying that Pierre Cartier had arrived from France with documents concerning the Hope diamond which he wished to show them. What Cartier actually did was to hand Mrs. McLean the Hope diamond and ask her if she would keep it over the weekend. (Cartier's, in the meantime, had put it in a new mounting.)

Sometime over the weekend Mrs. McLean began to want the diamond and agreed to buy it, although months went by before a contract was signed. Like many less wealthy people, she traded in some of her jewelry toward the purchase price, and then bought it on the installment plan.

In her book she wrote that, because of the superstitions surrounding the gem, she didn't let her friends or children touch it. This may have been true at first, but her son Jock said that he was teethed on the Hope diamond.[16] Soon after she bought the diamond, Mrs. McLean took it to a priest to have it blessed. From that day on, she said, she wore the diamond as a charm. Still, she was ambivalent about it. On the one hand, she thought it was a lucky stone for her. On the other hand, whenever any bad luck befell her, she always thought of the diamond.

Over the years, Mrs. McLean and the Hope diamond became almost inseparable. There is a story told that when she was about to have a goiter operation (to be done at her home), it was only with the greatest difficulty that the surgeon persuaded her to remove the necklace. She was always photographed wearing the Hope, frequently along with a number of other jewels. A typical photograph shows her wearing three necklaces at one time (the Hope on its diamond-studded chain, the Star of the East on another necklace, and a third necklace of diamond-studded links), diamond earrings, a pair of diamond clips, and a wristful of bracelets.

Once, when she was asked why she wore so much jewelry, she said, "If I take out one or two pieces to put on when I dress up I might as well put it all on and then I know where it is."[17]

To get a feeling for how much jewelry Mrs. McLean liked to wear, here is a list of the pieces she took with her on a trip to Russia in 1934 (taken from a customs declaration):

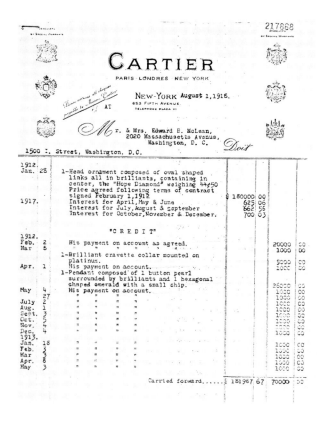

2 diamond clips

4 diamond bracelets

1 diamond chain with large white diamond and ruby

1 pr diamond earrings

1 large blue diamond known as Hope

1 long chain of sapphires and two large emeralds

1 short chain of sapphires and large emerald

1 pr emerald earrings

1 diamond cigarette case

1 pr black and white pendant earrings

1 diamond and pearl bracelet

1 pearl bracelet with diamond fountain

1 set turquoise chain and earrings

1 ruby and diamond bracelet

A 1918 Cartier statement to the McLeans discloses the terms of sale of the Hope diamond.

Letters and various papers once belonging to the McLeans are now in the Library of Congress. After hours spent looking through these papers, one begins to feel that being wealthy might be more of a burden than a joy. There are so many things to see to—several residences to furnish, decorate, repair, and alter; clothes for so many different events; the arrangements for renting private railroad cars, buying horses, resetting jewelry; arranging for insurance, entertainment for parties, etc., etc. The clothbound set of the *Encyclopaedia Britannica* must be sent back to be bound in sheepskin. Even a hunting trip culminates in correspondence with Abercrombie and

Fitch over how to use the horns and hides of the moose. "The feet of the moose," that venerable store advised, "can be used in making a very neat hatrack and one that you are not apt to duplicate anywhere."

Stories were told about how Mrs. McLean would pawn the Hope diamond when she needed ready cash. In their book *Hockshop*, William and Florence Simpson described one such episode. The Simpson shop was in New York, but at Mrs. McLean's request the Simpsons came to Washington to the McLean home, "Friendship." Simpson describes Mrs. McLean as small and very thin; she was then about forty-seven years old. When she entered the room, he asked to see the Hope. "She looked blank for a moment, then said uncertainly, 'What did I do with that necklace?' "[18] A maid was sent to look for the diamond, and in the meantime the three talked until Mrs. McLean suddenly remembered that 'Mike' had it. Going to the window she called, 'Mike! Here Mike!'

"The next moment a reddish Great Dane bounded into the room. Twisted around his neck was one of the most ornate diamond necklaces I had ever seen. I stared, unbelievingly, as Mrs. McLean bent over, patted him and unfastened the necklace.

"Because it was—my God!—the Hope diamond."[19]

And then, Simpson said, he wondered how many of her much-publicized pets were wearing other jewels.

In her autobiography Mrs. McLean said, "My own preference, generally, is for show. I should have been quite willing, if anyone had proposed it, to be married while hanging by my knees from the crosspiece of the spire of any well-known church. If I had a dog, I wanted him to be a dog people turned to stare at; it was the same with any of my possessions, and with many of my acts."[20]

It is quite possible that the scene of Mike wearing the Hope was staged completely for the Simpsons' benefit. Mrs. McLean liked being different, being talked about, being a little outrageous. She enhanced the legend of the Hope diamond. She also could be a generous, warm-hearted woman, especially to individuals whose misfortunes came to her personal attention. She fed the members of the Bonus Army, entertained World War II soldiers, set up the Walsh Club for War Workers, even took an evicted veteran, his wife, and their three children into her home until they could find a place to live.

She entertained lavishly and often; her New Year's Eve parties and Easter breakfasts were annual events. She was strong on good manners and good behavior. Anyone who drank too much and became unruly was not asked again.

In later years Mrs. McLean let many people touch, hold, or try on the Hope diamond. Probably no other famous diamond has been worn or handled by so many people now living. Nannie Chase, Mrs. McLean's secretary for seven years, said that every Wednesday, Mrs. McLean, wearing the Hope diamond, would visit wounded World War II soldiers at Walter Reed Army Hospital and actually let some of the soldiers play catch with the diamond.

Many brides wear something borrowed and something blue at their weddings, but for a woman living today in Ripley, New York, that something was the Hope diamond. When the bride, a former Navy WAVE, married an amputee in 1945, Mrs. McLean

A youthful Evalyn Walsh McLean wears the Hope diamond mounted as a head ornament.

Evalyn Walsh McLean wears the Hope diamond in a picture which she especially approved for publication.

lent her the Hope diamond for the ceremony.

Beatrice Meyerson, at present a volunteer tour guide at the Smithsonian, wore the Hope diamond when she was a little girl. Her parents were invited to a party at the McLean estate, and took Beatrice with them. Wanting to entertain her young guest, Mrs. McLean fastened the Hope on its diamond chain around her neck. Beatrice remembers that she was quite a bit older before she found out that all diamonds aren't blue.

So far in this account, Mrs. McLean's life has seemed gay and interesting, but she had more than her share of troubles. In addition to the tragic early death of her brother Vinson, her first-born son, also named Vinson, died as a result of an automobile accident when he was nine years old. Mrs. McLean took refuge in morphine for short periods following the deaths of her brother and her father, but she was able to break away from the habit. Ned McLean had a long romance with another woman and tried many times to secure a divorce from his wife. He also drank heavily, and eventually was declared insane and was confined to Sheppard and Enoch Pratt Hospital in Towson, Maryland, until his death in 1941. Even in insanity, wealth made a difference: he was not housed in the main building but lived in a separate cottage on the hospital grounds. In 1946 Mrs. McLean's only daughter, Evalyn McLean Reynolds, died from an overdose of sleeping pills when she was only twenty-five. Mrs. McLean never recovered from this blow and died of pneumonia on April 26, 1947.

An incredible number of people seem to have been at her bedside when she died, according to the newspapers. The names read like the guest list for a dinner party. There were Dr. Barnard J. Walsh, her physician; Father Edmund A. Walsh, vice-president of Georgetown University; Mrs. Eleanor Patterson, publisher of the *Washington Times Herald*; Supreme Court Justice Frank Murphy; Miss Eleanor Baumgartner, Justice Murphy's secretary; Judge Thurman Arnold; Mrs. Arnold; Frank C. Waldrop, *Times-Herald* editorial writer; Robert R. Reynolds, Mrs. McLean's son-in-law; and Nannie Chase, her secretary.

In her will Mrs. McLean requested that her jewelry be held in trust until the youngest of her grandchildren at the time the will was drawn (Mamie Spears Reynolds, then four) had reached the age of twenty-five. It was then to be divided among those

A model wears the Hope diamond with the Star of the East diamond suspended from it. Her earrings, bracelets, and rings also formerly belonged to Evalyn Walsh McLean.

and any future grandchildren. Had it been possible to observe her wishes, the jewelry would have been distributed in 1968. Two years after Mrs. McLean's death, however, the court granted a petition of the executor, trustees, and the family to sell the jewels to pay debts and claims against the estate. In the official appraisal, the Hope was valued at $176,920 and the pear-shaped Star of the East diamond at $185,000. In addition to these, there were seventy-two other pieces of jewelry. The whole collection was sold to New York jeweler Harry Winston. At the time, the newspapers gave an approximate purchase price of one and a quarter million dollars, but a recent book, *Wills, A Dead Giveaway* by Millie Considine and Ruth Pool, lists the price Winston paid as $611,500.

A GIFT TO THE NATION

Soon after Winston purchased the Hope diamond, Mrs. Thomas Phipps, a New York society leader, wore it at a charity ball at the Ritz-Carlton Hotel—the Bal de Tête, held November 16, 1949. This was the first of many such occasions. During the nine years Harry Winston owned the Hope diamond, it traveled thousands of miles and was used to raise millions of dollars for charity.

Winston had often expressed the wish that the United States might develop a major national jewel collection. He began to discuss with Smithsonian Institution officials the possibility of donating the Hope diamond to the museum to serve as the focal point for such a collection and also as a stimulus to other potential donors. Arrangements were concluded in 1958, and the announcement that the Hope diamond would be given to the Smithsonian rated a banner headline in the *Washington Post*. Winston's goal of an important gem collection for the United States is being realized as other donors have made major contributions. The collection now includes magnificent jewelry; some, like the favorite diamond earrings of France's Marie Antoinette and the diamond nuptial crown worn by the last three czarinas of Russia, once belonged to the crown jewels of their countries.

The Hope diamond was formally presented to the Smithsonian on November 10, 1958. Sent from New York in a plain brown package by registered mail, the diamond was insured for a million dollars while in transit. It was delivered by postman James

The formal presentation of the Hope diamond to the Smithsonian Institution, November 10, 1958. From left to right: Mrs. Harry Winston, wife of the donor; the late Leonard Carmichael, Secretary of the Smithsonian; and Dr. George S. Switzer, then Curator of Mineralogy.

G. Todd to the Gem Room of the Natural History Building, where quite an assemblage awaited. The then Secretary of the Smithsonian, the late Leonard Carmichael; Mrs. Harry Winston, wife of the donor; Dr. George S. Switzer, Curator of Mineralogy; Postmaster General Arthur E. Summerfield; and high government officials and persons prominent in Washington society had all gathered for the occasion. Winston himself, under the terms of his insurance policy, could not be photographed, and so was not present.

Dr. Carmichael opened the package and gave it to Mrs. Winston, who then made the formal presentation. Meanwhile, armed Smithsonian guards, Washington metropolitan policemen, and postal inspectors stood by for security purposes.

After the presentation ceremonies, Dr. Switzer put the Hope into its new home, a safe in the Gem Room. Closed at night, the door to the safe is opened during exhibit hours, enabling visitors to get a good view of the diamond through a glass cover. For the sake of security, the glass is more than one inch thick. This, unfortunately, cuts down the effective brilliance of the diamond by about 25 percent. Soon after the Hope was given to the Smithsonian it was carefully examined by museum curators. The results of this examination, and physical descriptions of the Hope, are given on page 62.

Newspapers all over the country noted the arrival of the Hope diamond at the Smithsonian. Most of their accounts paid special attention to the bad luck which is supposed to accompany it. The *Washington Post* remarked, "and as of Monday, if anyone is hexed, it will not be [Winston] but the staff of the Smithsonian Institution!" A cartoonist drew a battered Uncle Sam wearing the Hope and muttering, "That's all I need!"

In the Hope diamond's first three days on display, there were 9,504 visitors to the museum, as compared to 5,519 for the same period the week before.

The Hope diamond has left the National Museum of Natural History only twice since it first took up residence there in 1958.

In 1962 the Hope was taken to Paris for an exhibition at the Louvre museum called "Ten Centuries of French Jewelry." There, it was displayed with two famous diamonds, the Regent and the Sancy, and with the Côte de Bretagne, which is a red spinel carved in the shape of a dragon. If it is true, as many experts believe, that the Hope diamond was recut from a blue diamond formerly among the French royal jewels (a theory discussed later in this book), this exhibition marked the first reunion of these gems in 170 years.

The Smithsonian had refused the first request to lend the Hope to the Louvre. Museum officials were reluctant to deprive Smithsonian visitors of a view of the diamond for a month during the spring, always an especially busy time. They were also concerned for the safety of the diamond. The decision to lend the Hope was ultimately made through the intervention of Mrs. Jacqueline Kennedy, who had been approached by André Malraux, French Minister of Culture. In a gracious response to the loan of the Hope diamond, the Louvre later permitted Leonardo da Vinci's Mona Lisa to be exhibited in Washington at the National Gallery of Art.

The courier who took the Hope diamond to the Louvre, Dr. Switzer of the Department of Mineral Sciences, had an uncommonly difficult time getting there. His plane was so damaged in a rough landing in Philadelphia that the flight was canceled and he had to take another flight to New York. The plane from New York to Frankfurt, Germany, was an hour and a half late departing, and there was still another four-hour delay in Frankfurt. He finally arrived in Paris about nine hours behind schedule and, no doubt, with some thought about the "curse" of the Hope diamond. The telegram to the museum announcing his safe arrival said, "Mission accomplished."

The Hope diamond's second trip was to South Africa, in 1965, for a special Easter show. This time the telegram announced, "Switzer and Baby Doll arrived safely." While the diamond was away, a replica was put in its place in the Hall of Gems.

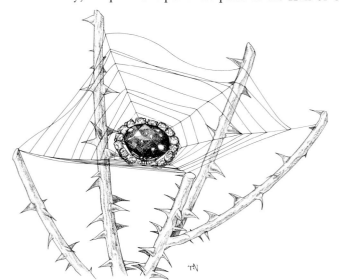

The Hope diamond was displayed on a gold rosebush in a 1965 exhibition in South Africa. In keeping with its legend of bad luck, the diamond rested in the center of a golden web, like a fat blue spider.

Sets of glass replicas of famous diamonds are common, and a replica of the Hope—although usually an inaccurate one—is included in most sets. In a special exhibit of synthetic gems at the Smithsonian Institution in 1973, a particularly beautiful copy of the Hope diamond, complete with mounting and chain, was shown. It was set entirely with stones cut from a relatively new man-made diamond substitute called YAG (yttrium aluminum garnet).

The necklace which the chairman of the Hope Ball wears at that annual event to benefit "Project Hope" is a copy presented to the project by Harry Winston, Inc. The Hope is represented by a model made of synthetic blue spinel, and white spinels are used in place of the small white diamonds in the setting. Harry Winston, Inc., has valued this necklace at $25,000.

A dramatization of episodes from the diamond's story, "The Legendary Curse of the Hope Diamond," was presented on national television in March 1975, with Bradford Dillman and Samantha Eggar portraying Edward and Evalyn McLean, and with Rod Serling as narrator. Those who will not relinquish the belief that the Hope diamond does bear a curse may have their conviction reinforced by the death of Serling, following open heart surgery, less than six months after the completion of the program. He was fifty years old.

Bradford Dillman and Samantha Eggar portrayed Edward and Evalyn McLean in a Smithsonian television special, "The Legendary Curse of the Hope Diamond," presented March 27, 1975.

Speculations about the Hope

Edwin W. Streeter, a London jeweler, was aware that the French crown jewels had included, until their theft in 1792, a blue diamond which was then considered unique. When it was stolen, the French blue weighed 67⅛ carats. Streeter reasoned that the diamond would have been recut to disguise its origin and that the recutting could logically have produced a 44½-carat brilliant such as the Hope and a six- to seven-carat drop-shape diamond. One side of the Hope is straighter than the other, and it seemed to Streeter that the larger diamond could have been cleaved along this plane. (If the French blue was cut to produce the Hope, it must have been cleaved rather than sawed because the art of sawing around 1792 was too tedious to permit the sawing of a diamond the size of the French blue.)

According to Streeter's theory, the final piece of the puzzle appeared in 1874 at the sale of the jewel collection which had belonged to William, the Duke of Brunswick (grandson of the first Duke, Charles William Ferdinand, who had formed the collection). Included in the sale was a small blue drop-shaped diamond of about six carats. Streeter said that he had an opportunity to examine this diamond and the Hope side by side and he found them to be of the same color and quality. He concluded that the Hope diamond had once been part of the French blue. The above account is recorded in his book *Precious Stones and Gems*, published in 1877. Also, C. W. King, in *The Natural History of Gems*, printed in 1867, said, "Hope's blue diamond was supposed by Barbot to be that of the French regalia stolen in 1792."

Although there is no scientific proof, the unusual size and color of the diamonds involved constitute strong circumstantial evidence which has led most writers to assume that the Hope was cut from the French blue diamond.

Yet it is still possible to have doubts. One question centers on Streeter's comparison of the color of the two diamonds. If they came from the same diamond and weighed 44½ carats and 6½ carats, they would *not* look identical in color. The larger diamond would appear to be a deeper blue because of its greater depth. We cannot know what Streeter actually saw. It is possible that he called identical two colors of differing intensities but whose quality was the same, in which case he may well have been looking at two pieces of the French blue. If, however, the diamonds' colors were in fact of the same intensity, then Streeter's theory of the Hope's origin is suspect.

Some other disconcerting evidence is available. In addition to *Precious Stones and Gems*, Streeter wrote *The Great Diamonds of the World* (1882). His theory on the origin of the Hope is discussed in both books, as well as in their subsequent editions (there were at least six editions of *Precious Stones and Gems*). In each edition, the

An illustration from Edwin W. Streeter's 1882 edition of Precious Stones and Gems. *When Tavernier bought the blue diamond, it was already cut. The top drawing is Streeter's conception of what it was like in the rough. In the center, Streeter shows how he thinks the French blue diamond was cut into the Hope and Brunswick diamonds. The bottom drawing shows the Hope as it was mounted when Henry Philip Hope owned it, except for the pearl drop, which could have been added later.*

details concerning the Hope are different! In the 1877 edition, he wrote, "The purchaser put the stone [the Brunswick blue drop diamond] into my hands and I examined it in juxtaposition with the Hope diamond." He wrote in the 1882 edition, however, that the Brunswick blue diamond "fell into the hands of some competent judges, who examined it in juxtaposition with the Hope diamond. . . ."

Sometimes Streeter completely contradicts himself. In the 1877 edition of *Precious Stones and Gems*, Streeter stated, "Besides the Hope and Brunswick Diamonds, there are only three diamonds known in Europe that can justly be termed 'Blue' and these all differ from the 'Hope' and from each other in color." He then describes them as (1) a "Brilliant, also sold at the Duke's sale, a blue stone with a dash of jet in it, weighing 13¼ carats. It is of an octagon shape with 'flat top and a thick back' not unlike a Rose Diamond"; (2) "A very fine, but small dark Blue Brilliant, weighing about five grains" (which Streeter owned himself); and (3) a "Blue Brilliant in private hands which weighs about 4½ carats, is somewhat square in form and is paler in hue than its famous congeners."

Compare this with Streeter's account in the first edition (1882) of *The Great Diamonds of the World*. Here he said that the French blue was cut into three pieces rather than two. He then proceeded to describe the two smaller gems, and we find that the descriptions tally exactly with those given under (1) and (2) above. In other words, two diamonds which he earlier described as being different from the Hope and from each other in color were now said to have once been parts of the same diamond.

The contradictions are a mystery, but if one is to accept Streeter's theory at all, the first account, in which he suggests a recutting into two stones, the smaller one weighing six to seven carats, is the only one considered possible by modern diamond cutters. The Hope diamond was found in 1965 to be the only blue diamond known to phosphoresce red following exposure to ultraviolet light. If the Duke of Brunswick's smaller blue diamond could be found and tested in this way, it would be possible to either strengthen or demolish his theory.

Large blue diamonds are so rare that it is logical to assume that the Hope diamond was cut from the French blue in order to conceal the fact that it had been stolen. Only one other large blue diamond was known in Europe during the seventeenth and eighteenth centuries and this, the 35.32-carat Wittelsbach blue, has a recorded history for this period.

THE HISTORY OF THE FRENCH BLUE DIAMOND

The known history of the French blue diamond begins about 1642, and is itself material enough for many novels. Travel, riches, revolution, and a daring robbery—all are a part of the saga of this stone.

It was in approximately 1642 that a blue diamond weighing 112³⁄₁₆ carats was purchased by Jean Baptiste Tavernier in India, then the only known source of diamonds. It is believed to have come from the Kollur Mine in Golconda.

Tavernier (1605-1689) was a French traveler and jewel merchant. His father was

Jean Baptiste Tavernier, French traveler and jewel merchant, who bought the 112 3/16-carat blue diamond in India and sold it to Louis XIV. He is wearing the robe of honor given him by an Indian ruler.

a mapmaker, and Tavernier was inspired to visit all the countries he saw on his father's maps. Between 1631 and 1668 he made six voyages to Persia and India, buying and selling jewels as he traveled. When Tavernier returned to France in December 1668, he was the object of general curiosity, and Louis XIV ordered him presented at court. He brought with him a number of diamonds which he showed the King, who was so pleased with them that he bought, in addition to the blue diamond which is described as being the most beautiful of them all, forty-four large diamonds and 1,122 smaller ones. The total price was 897,731 livres (about $180,000), of which 220,000 livres were for the blue diamond.

In February 1669, in consideration of his services to France, the King granted Tavernier certain letters which conferred upon him a title of nobility, after which he purchased the Barony of Aubonne in Switzerland.

When the blue diamond was purchased it was Indian-cut. The Indians valued size in a diamond rather than brilliance, and the facets were often placed only as necessary to remove or conceal flaws. Tavernier wrote that in India the stones were often cut right at the mines. In order to increase the brilliance of the diamond, the King in 1673 ordered his diamond cutter, Sieur Pitau, to recut the gem. When recut, it was triangular in shape (sometimes described as heart- or drop-shaped) and weighed 67⅛ carats. It was then officially named the "Blue Diamond of the Crown." (G. F. Herbert Smith in his book *Gemstones* raises the possibility that a second, smaller blue diamond could have resulted from this cutting.) After the diamond was cut, it was placed in a simple pronged setting made of gold and enameled on the back. It remained in this mounting until 1749.

The diamonds bought from Tavernier were only one of many purchases of diamonds and jewelry made by Louis XIV. In *A History of the Crown Jewels of Europe* (1960), Lord Twining wrote, "During the reign of Louis XIV the French crown jewels were the finest and richest collection of gem stones as yet found in Europe and probably in the world."

Crown jewels in other countries were not always all they seemed to be. In England, for example, it was often found necessary to rent precious stones to use in the coronation regalia. For the coronation of George II in 1727, not only were diamonds hired to adorn the crowns but, in addition, Queen Caroline rented jewels worth £100,000 to decorate her petticoat, "which was so immensely stiff and heavy that she could not kneel down and it was, therefore, fitted with pulleys to draw it up like a curtain."[21]

It was during the reign of Louis XIV that diamonds first superseded pearls in importance, and were used in profusion. "Diamond rivieres (a necklace consisting of a single row of graduated diamonds) took the place of strings of pearls."[22] Royal fam-

A drawing of twenty of the most important diamonds sold to Louis XIV by Tavernier. In the upper left-hand corner are three views of the Indian-cut blue diamond, described here as a "faire violet" in color.

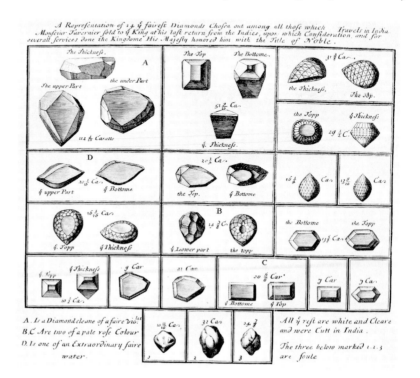

Louis XIV, the "Sun King," is radiant in his frock coat liberally embellished with diamond buttons and jeweled buttonholes. He purchased the blue diamond from Tavernier in 1668 or 1669.

ilies had so many diamonds that their subjects found it difficult to explain where they all came from, but they tried. An early writer reported in all seriousness that a lady from a noble family possessed two diamonds, heirlooms, which frequently produced small diamonds so that whoever inspected them at certain fixed intervals could see them giving birth.

After his wife, Marie Thérèse, died, Louis XIV had nearly all of her jewels reset for his own use. Men then wore knee breeches and shirts with long ruffled sleeves. Over the shirt was worn a waistcoat or vest and then a frock coat extending to just above the knee. These were lavishly decorated with jeweled buttons and buttonholes as well as buttonhole ornaments. The kind and number of buttonholes were indications of the rank of the wearer. Louis XIV had two complete sets of diamond ornaments. One set contained 123 diamond buttons and 396 jeweled buttonholes. Obviously, not all the buttonholes were functional. This set also had a hat ornament of seven diamonds, a spray to wear on the outer coat, and a cross. The other set was even more elaborate, and there was a third set with pearl ornaments. He also had diamond-studded garters and double shoe buckles and a sword set with 131 diamonds. An engraving of Louis on this page shows how it was possible for him to wear so many diamonds at the same time.

The French blue diamond was used in various ways in the costumes of Louis XIV and Louis XV. W. R. Cattelle describes one such use which involved Louis XIV: "... it is recorded that the King wore a large blue diamond suspended from a ribbon around the neck when he decked himself with jewels estimated at 12,000,000 livres (roughly £1,000,000) to receive the Persian Ambassador at his court in February 1715."[23]

Louis XIV introduced the use of jewels in the insignia of the orders of chivalry, which had previously been only of gold and silver, either plain or enameled. After his great grandson, Louis XV, became king, this custom was continued. In December 1749 Louis XV ordered Jacquemin, the crown jeweler, to design a decoration of the Order of the Golden Fleece and to set in it the Côte de Bretagne and the Blue Diamond of the Crown (French blue).

The Côte de Bretagne, originally thought to be a ruby, was one of three large red spinels in the French crown jewels. (Red spinels are sometimes confusingly referred to as balas rubies.) All three were of irregular shape and were subsequently recut. The Côte de Bretagne was the only survivor of the jewels which formed the treasure of the crown in 1530.

Jacquemin ordered Jacques Guay, a carver of gems who had often been employed by Madame de Pompadour, to cut the Côte de Bretagne in the form of a dragon in such a way as to conceal three holes in the stone. In recutting, the Côte de Bretagne dropped from 206 carats to 105 carats, but the result, a dragon carved in oriental style, was greatly admired.

In addition to the Côte de Bretagne and the blue diamond, the completed decoration of the Order of the Golden Fleece contained a six-sided brilliant-cut diamond which, according to Streeter, weighed 31¾ carats. This made a decoration considered a masterpiece of the jeweler's art as well as an object of great value. It was the practice of the jewelers to the French crown in the seventeenth and eighteenth centuries to

The famous Côte de Bretagne jewel, which was set in the Order of the Golden Fleece with the French blue diamond. Shaped like the head and body of a dragon, this red spinel is now in the Galerie d'Apollon at the Louvre in Paris.

Front and back views of the Order of the Golden Fleece made for Louis XV. The central stone is the red spinel, known as the Côte de Bretagne, carved in the shape of a dragon's head and body. It is set with the head down. Gold and topaz flames issue from the dragon's mouth and partially encircle the French blue diamond at the bottom of the decoration. The tail, made of gold and set with diamonds, is coiled upward and around the hexagonal brilliant and then goes through the gold loop at the top. The ribbon of the Order was meant to be threaded through the loop.

make lead castings of all the jewelry mounted. Thus the illustrations·shown at left of the Fleece, as mounted by Jacquemin, were done from the lead models of the original and represent the design exactly, even though the Golden Fleece was broken up. The Fleece was part of the King's regalia.

Louis XV died in 1774 and was succeeded by his grandson, Louis XVI. It is related, as part of the legend of the Hope diamond, that Louis XVI's queen, Marie Antoinette, wore the Hope (French blue) diamond. According to Twining, however, the French blue remained in the Order of the Golden Fleece, which was worn only by the King. Louis XVI had two chief sets of jewels, one white and one colored, each containing an Order of the Golden Fleece. One set was made entirely of gold and diamonds, valued at 413,000 livres; the other, valued at 3,394,000 livres, was the Golden Fleece, set with the Côte de Bretagne and the blue diamond. The blue diamond alone was estimated to be worth three million livres (about $600,000). With this, Louis wore a diamond epaulette and a jewel-studded sword.

The unrest which preceded the French Revolution had already begun in 1775. To emphasize how oblivious Louis XVI seemed to be to the events of his reign, his diary is often quoted. A dedicated hunter, he frequently gave the day's bag of game the main place in his diary. On the day the Bastille fell, the sole entry in his diary is "Nothing."

In 1789, the year historically marking the start of the revolution, the Constituent Assembly passed a law which made the crown jewels available only for the use of the reigning king. Louis XVI and Marie Antoinette kept some of the jewels until 1791. On June 20 of that year, after months of indecision, the royal couple tried to flee the country. They were apprehended the following day and returned under guard to Paris. The crown jewels were taken from them and placed in the Garde-Meuble, a sort of combination museum and furniture storehouse, which also contained the arms and armor of French kings and a collection of tapestries and other precious objects.

Alarmed by rumors of a project to carry off the crown jewels, the revolutionary government had a new inventory of them made on June 25, 1791. The matter of their ultimate disposition was considered. On the twenty-eighth of September, 1791, the government decided not to alter or sell the jewels at that time, and to continue to house them in the Garde-Meuble.

Meanwhile, although Marie Antoinette no longer had any of the crown jewels, she had been able to keep some of the jewelry she had brought to France as a bride in 1770, according to an account by her hairdresser, Leonard. In his privately printed memoirs, Leonard described how Marie Antoinette, late in 1791, entrusted him with a shagreen leather casket, instructing him to sell the jewels it contained in London because she and Louis XVI were desperately in need of money. She made a point of telling Leonard that these jewels had never cost France a penny.

Leonard left Paris on December 27, 1791, with the jewelry concealed in his luggage. He had taken the precaution of having it appraised first, and the value given was 350,000 livres (about $70,000). Arriving in London on December 30, Leonard went to a jeweler in the Strand, having first looked up a former girl friend to be his inter-

48

Hortensia—a pink diamond of 20 carats, probably purchased from Tavernier by Louis XIV at the same time as the blue diamond and mentioned in the 1791 inventory of the French crown jewels. It is now on display at the Louvre.

preter. Upon seeing the pieces, the jeweler noted that the stones had been set in Germany at a much earlier date. He must have been a very honest man (Leonard says he was "a true gentleman, that is, an Englishman,")[24] for he pointed out that the stones were partly hidden by the settings and weighed more than they appeared to. He paid Leonard 100,000 livres more than the appraised value, and Leonard delivered the money to the correspondent Marie Antoinette had designated.

Jewels have definitely been an asset in troubled times in the past. What other form of property worth so much money could have been so easily smuggled out of France?

THE THEFT OF THE CROWN JEWELS

In August 1792, after the French royal family had been imprisoned in the Tower, the Minister of the Interior proposed to the National Assembly that the crown jewels be sold and the money used to back the paper currency. At about this time certain thieves decided that if the crown jewels were to be dispersed anyway, they might as well assist in the process and profit from it.

If one were to write a play about the robbery of the French crown jewels and the events surrounding it, no one would believe it. The details of the account given here were taken from a book by Germain Bapst, *Histoire des Joyaux de la Couronne de France*, printed in 1889.

As background, the Garde-Meuble was very poorly guarded. The man in charge of the treasure, one Thierry, had complained and warned his superior about this on numerous occasions, but no improvements were made. If the relief guards were late, the guards on duty often wouldn't wait for them, leaving the Garde-Meuble unpro-tected.

A thief named Paul Miette conceived the plan to rob the Garde-Meuble, according to Bapst. In the midst of his planning he was arrested for another burglary and put in the prison at La Force, where he used his time to enlist a number of the other prisoners in the projected robbery. The enterprise was further aided by the massacres of September 1792, which plunged Paris into chaos, for highwaymen, professional robbers, receivers of stolen goods, cutpurses, and convicts of all kinds were released from prison. The police were helpless. Some criminals even disguised themselves as municipal officers and stopped citizens from the country, demanding their watch chains or their shoe buckles as a so-called offering to the country.

Every night, thieves were able to enter the Palace of the Tuileries and penetrate to the innermost rooms, from which they carried away precious objects. These thefts were known and yet were repeated without fear of punishment. The only way to stop this constant depredation, notes a police report from this period, would be to wall up all the windows, skylights, and other openings of the palace.

The National Guard had the duty of protecting the public monuments, so they were assigned to the Garde-Meuble. The jewels were in a room on the first floor of that building, most of them stored in eight boxes that had been placed in the drawers of a marquetry cabinet with a hidden lock. There also was a copper-bound walnut jewel case with handles, in which the decorations and buttons of the King were kept. Since this box was too big to go in a drawer, it was left on a porphyry table in the middle of the room.

Meanwhile, Paul Miette and his accomplices, among them Cadet Guillot from Rouen, had recruited friends from the provinces to assist in the robbery. The project involved about fifty individuals, grouped in several bands drawn from all parts of France.

On September 11, 1792, at 11:00 p.m. some of those involved in the plot met in the Place de la Concorde. The more agile forced a window in the Garde-Meuble, cutting the glass with a diamond cutter and reaching through to open the window. The heavy iron bars with which each window was provided were not in place, a bit of luck for the intruders.

Once inside, their first care was to close the doors that led to the internal staircase by which the guards posted at the bottom of the court could have entered. The thieves used tapes secured by seals to close the doors, since their judicial character was likely to discourage anyone from entering casually. The lack of sentinels just outside made the conspirators feel secure. They had only one fear: that their noise would attract the National Guard and that the guard would not hesitate to break the seals and enter. Just in case, they added iron hooks to wedge the doors shut, hoping at least for time to escape.

The thieves went first to the glass cases containing the mounted jewelry that they had studied earlier when the collections were still open to the public. According to Bapst, also stolen on this night were the King's ornaments in the box on the porphyry table. The thieves left about 2:00 a.m.

Though many jewels still remained in the Garde-Meuble, the thieves stayed away the following day, September 12, but a larger number went back on September 13 to find the window still unbarred. This time, they removed small boxes filled with diamonds. It was probably on this night that the Regent and Sancy diamonds were taken. Still undiscovered, the thieves waited through September fourteenth, but went back again on the fifteenth. Each time they went back, more people were involved. By now there were so many that they didn't all know each other. After the robbery on the night of the fifteenth, part of the band met at a café and fought over the spoils of the expedition. Two of the thieves went down by the Seine to divide their loot, and there they sold one of their boxes of gems to a passerby. This man, upon taking his purchase to a pawnbroker, was advised to report the matter to the authorities. Together, he and the pawnbroker went to the police on the morning of the sixteenth. After having been notified, the police checked the inner doors of the Garde-Meuble, found the seals still intact—and went away satisfied.

On the evening of the sixteenth, the thieves went back once more. By this time there were fifty robbers, half of them women friends. Some were in the costume of the National Guard. They took wine and food and organized a supper.

The theft was finally discovered early on September seventeenth. Most of the robbers had fled, and only a few were arrested. When the police entered the room, they found many small diamonds on the floor along with pearls and burglars' tools. The crown jewels had been valued at 30,000,000 francs; what was left was worth only about 5,500 francs.

A large part of these crown jewels had been buried under a tree and were recovered almost immediately with the aid of informants. The Regent diamond was found much later, hidden in an attic, and the Guise and several other diamonds were also eventually recovered.

The comic opera aspects of the affair didn't stop with the discovery of the robbery. No one involved seems to have considered the possibility that the robbery was purely for monetary gain. The Revolutionary Tribunal saw it as a plot to overthrow the government, and the thieves they caught were charged with treason instead of theft. Madame Roland, wife of the Minister of the Interior, accused Danton and Fabre d'Eglantine. According to Fabre d'Eglantine, the Girondins were the true robbers. Marat accused the aristocrats and the public prosecutor of the Revolutionary Tribunal said he saw the hand of Marie Antoinette in the matter.

Another elaborate plot was suggested at the time and has been advanced occasionally through the years. The Duke of Brunswick was in command of Austrian and Prussian troops fighting the French with the avowed purpose of rescuing Louis XVI and Marie Antoinette. The military advantage seemed to be with the Duke; so, when he inexplicably retreated a few days after the robbery, it was thought that government officials might have staged the robbery, thereby enabling them to give the Duke a large portion of the crown jewels as a bribe to withdraw his troops. The fact that so many of the jewels were soon recovered discredits this theory. Stanley Loomis, however, in his book *The Fatal Friendship*[25] (which details Marie Antoinette's relationship to the

Swedish count, Axel Fersen) suggests that Brunswick was bribed with the blue diamond alone.

Some books say that the stolen blue diamond was sold to the Spanish royal family. As proof, they offer a portrait of Maria Luisa of Spain painted by Goya in 1799. This painting, which is now in the Taft Museum in Cincinnati, Ohio, shows Maria Luisa wearing an elaborate necklace with a large blue stone in the center. Normally, one would assume it to be a sapphire. The only reason for thinking otherwise arises from the circumstance that the Sancy diamond, also stolen from the French crown jewels, appeared in Spain in 1808. That the story about one diamond may become identified with another, however, is illustrated by an isolated report that the blue diamond had been purchased by an agent of the Demidoff family in Russia. This actually happened to the Sancy, but at a later date (1828).

A close examination of the necklace in Goya's painting shows a stone which appears to be significantly larger than the Hope diamond. Since virtually all other stories place the diamond in England, a Spanish chapter in its history seems unlikely.

According to Bapst, the thief Cadet Guillot probably took the Order of the Golden Fleece, in which the French blue diamond and the dragon-shaped spinel, the Côte de Bretagne, were mounted, during the first robbery on September 11. Cadet Guillot left Paris that night. Instead of returning to his home in Rouen, he went to Nantes and took the boat to Le Havre. He stayed there for a time and then went to London. In both these cities, he is reported to have shown jewels in a morocco case. Bapst says the Fleece was broken up in London and the blue diamond cut in two pieces there. How Guillot disposed of it is not known.

That Guillot would have gone to London is logical. Mawe wrote in 1813 that the London market had three main sources for diamonds at that time: India, Brazil—and refugees from the French revolution. "The next great influx was at the time of the French revolution. The nobility and other emigrants who sought shelter here from the commotions of their own country brought with them large quantities of Diamonds. These, from the necessities of their owners, soon found their way to market, and were disposed of to the jewellers at prices which had a reference rather to the necessity of the sellers, than to the intrinsic value of the article; for the regular sale price of Diamonds did not suffer the smallest abatement on this account."[26]

The Côte de Bretagne turned up in Germany in 1796 in the possession of an emigré named Lancry, who is supposed to have been commissioned by Guillot to sell it. Shortly afterward, it disappeared a second time. This gem is now in the Louvre but no one is sure how it was returned, although it is thought to have been acquired by Louis XVIII.

Twenty years separate the disappearance of the French blue diamond in 1792 from the first appearance of the blue diamond that was to be purchased by Henry Philip Hope. An additional gap in the Hope's history occurs much later, between 1901 and 1908. Until all the facts are known, the Hope diamond will continue to be a tantalizing mystery.

Evaluating the Legend

Anyone who has read articles about the Hope diamond will have noticed that some stories usually included in the history of the Hope have been omitted in this account. All untrue or unsubstantiated episodes have been excluded from the narrative. Instead, these accounts are listed below, and, following each one, an attempt is made to evaluate its accuracy.

1. *Jean Baptiste Tavernier, French traveler and gem merchant who acquired the blue diamond in India, is said to have stolen the diamond from an idol's eye. He is supposed later to have lost his fortune through his son's or nephew's mismanagement or theft, and, on a trip to Russia to recoup his fortunes, is said to have been torn apart by wild dogs.*

Tavernier was a merchant who made repeated trips to the same locations. He had a reputation to uphold. Because of Tavernier's honesty in paying the 2-percent duty required by a native ruler, he was given a robe of honor which consisted of a robe, mantle, waistband, and turban. With these facts as background, it seems unlikely that he would steal a diamond from an idol. It also seems unlikely, from the shape of the blue diamond as it was then cut, that the stone was ever used as an idol's eye. In the upper left-hand corner of the illustration on page 44 is a drawing of the blue diamond as it was then. In the upper right-hand corner is a diamond in the rose cut, which is much more appropriate for a stone meant to represent an eye, whether set normally or whether set in the forehead. (The famous Orloff diamond, which was originally an idol's eye, was cut in this way.)

It has been assumed that Tavernier was in financial difficulties, because he sold the land and barony of Aubonne in 1685. His most thorough biographer suggests, however, that he sold them because Frederick William, Elector of Brandenburg, had promised to make him the Elector's ambassador to India and had asked him to form a trading company. These plans collapsed, and in July 1687 Tavernier obtained a passport to Switzerland. He was in Copenhagen in 1688 or 1689, and one biographer reports that he died in Copenhagen. In 1876 his tomb was found in an old Protestant cemetery near Moscow. It is not known how he died, but, since he was eighty-four years old, his death could hardly be called premature or "unlucky." The first person to say that Tavernier was torn apart by wild dogs seems to have been the Cartier salesman who showed the Hope diamond to Mrs. McLean.

2. *Louis XIV died in agony and in disgrace, a fate supposedly attributable to wearing the diamond.*

Although some attribute his death to smallpox, Louis XIV died of gangrene. As reported in *The Sun King* by Nancy Mitford, he was in agony the last three weeks before his death. The disgrace probably refers to the internal problems over the weakening wars toward the end of his reign, which strained the economy of France, but France at his death was still a first-rate power.

3. *Louis XIV bestowed the blue diamond on his favorite, Madame de Montespan, and then almost immediately abandoned her.*

It is possible that Madame de Montespan wore the blue diamond. She arrived at court in 1660, and became the King's mistress in 1667. The blue diamond was purchased in 1669, recut and mounted (probably for the first time) in 1673. Madame de Montespan liked jewelry and often wore a great many diamonds.

During the French poisoning scandals, which began in 1676 and continued until 1682, many prominent people were involved—among them Madame de Montespan. It became known that she had gone to one of the accused for love philtres and other charms which she used on the King, and, judging from history, they seem to have been effective. She was also said to have participated in a Black Mass and to have had others said for her. The first poisoner to confess was the Marquise de Brinvilliers. "The whole of high society attended her trial and execution; she was beheaded and then burnt 'so that,' said Mme. de Sevigne wittily of the fire, 'we are all breathing her now.' "[27] The King apparently never believed that Madame de Montespan had ever poisoned anyone.

Nonetheless, she was gradually replaced in the King's affections by Madame Maintenon. Louis XIV turned Madame de Montespan out of her rooms next to his in December 1684.

4. *Nicholas Fouquet, Minister of Finance to Louis XIV, borrowed the blue diamond for a grand ball, and was executed by his king the next day.*

The incident of borrowing the diamond could not have happened. The ball referred to occurred on August 17, 1661, about seven and a half years before Louis XIV purchased the blue diamond. The day after the ball, Fouquet was imprisoned, but not executed.

5. *The beautiful Princess de Lamballe, who wore the blue diamond, was torn to pieces by a French mob.*

The Princess de Lamballe was a friend of Marie Antoinette rather than of her husband, Louis XVI. The blue diamond had been set in the Order of the Golden Fleece, an ornament intended to be worn by the King, in 1749, the same year the Princess de Lamballe was born. The diamond remained in this mounting until it was stolen in 1792, and there is no proof that the Princess ever wore it. She did, however, suffer the horrible death described.

6. *Louis XVI and Marie Antoinette, inheritors of the French blue diamond, went to the guillotine.*

That they went to the guillotine is true, of course, but probably only the King wore the diamond. Throughout the reign of Louis XVI, the diamond was mounted in the Order of the Golden Fleece, a part of the King's regalia. Both he and Marie Antoinette were sent to the guillotine; the King on January 21, 1793, and Marie Antoinette in

October of the same year. He was thirty-eight years old; she was thirty-seven.

7. *Wilhelm Fals, a Dutch diamond cutter, is said to have recut the French blue, producing a brilliant of 44½ carats. He then supposedly died of grief after his son, Hendrik, stole the diamond. As for Hendrik, he is said to have committed suicide in London in 1830.*

The cutter's name is sometimes given as Hals. No evidence has been found to support this story.

It is not known positively that the French blue diamond was recut, or, if it was, who did the cutting or whether the present Hope diamond was the result.

8. *François Beaulieu is said to have obtained the diamond from "a nameless suicide," presumably Hendrik Fals. Beaulieu was supposedly forced to sell it to Daniel Eliason for a fraction of its value—and then died the next day of starvation.*

In some versions of this story, Beaulieu was the one who brought the diamond from Amsterdam. In any case, the earliest mention I find of Beaulieu is in a book written by H. L. Gates, the source supposedly being the personal narrative of Lady Francis Hope (May Yohe). This book, called *The Mystery of the Hope Diamond*, was published in 1921. It contains many wholly fictional events and some glaring errors, beginning with the stealing of the blue diamond by Tavernier in 1588—but that date is seventeen years before Tavernier was born.

9. *The entire Hope family suffered assorted scandals, and the last of the once-wealthy Hopes was a bankrupt.*

Henry Philip Hope, the first of the family to own the diamond, had no notable misfortunes. Henry Thomas Hope, the second owner, seems to have led a normal and fairly prominent existence. He was a member of Parliament for many years. He did, however, die at the relatively young age of fifty-four. His widow had the Hope diamond until 1887 when, upon her death, an interest for life went to her grandson, Lord Francis Hope. He did indeed spend beyond his income, and became bankrupt in 1895. The estate was not lost, however, since his life interest had entitled him only to the income. He divorced May Yohe in 1902, and in 1904 married an Englishwoman by whom he had three children, one boy and two girls. His second wife died after only eight years of marriage, and one of their daughters died at age thirty-four. Lord Francis Hope himself, however, lived to be seventy-five. At sixty-two he had succeeded his older brother as Duke of Newcastle, presumably inheriting property as well as the title. Lord Francis was not the last of the family; his son is the present and ninth Duke of Newcastle.

10. *M. Jacques Colot, a French broker who bought the Hope from a New York dealer for 60,000 pounds sterling, was afflicted with madness and committed suicide.*

There are no facts available to substantiate this story, although a diamond dealer named M. Colot did exist.

11. *Prince Ivan Kanitovsky (variously described as a Russian and as an Eastern European prince) gave it or loaned it to a Folies Bergere actress named Lorens Ladue or Laduc. She was supposedly shot across the footlights on the next day by her lover— or by Prince Kanitovsky—as she wore the diamond. Prince Kanitovsky was stabbed to*

S. Dillon Ripley, Secretary of the Smithsonian Institution, smiles as he contemplates the Hope diamond. The Smithsonian staff does not subscribe to the supposed hex of the Hope diamond.

death by revolutionists.

No material has been found to substantiate either the episode or the existence of the actress and the prince.

12. *Simon Montharides, a Greek jeweler who sold the diamond to the Sultan of Turkey, was thrown over a precipice while riding in a car with his wife and child. All were killed.*

Again, no facts have been found to prove the story or the existence of the man.

Perhaps it is significant that, although each of these people is supposed to have owned the Hope diamond before Mrs. McLean did, no stories about them appeared in print until after the McLeans bought the diamond in 1911. In fact, no mention of bad luck or a curse associated with the Hope diamond has been found in any reference prior to 1910. This supports the belief of Paul Desautels, Curator of the Division of Mineralogy at the Smithsonian, that the stories of bad luck associated with the Hope diamond have a recent origin. While it is true, for example, that Louis XVI and Marie Antoinette owned the blue diamond and were guillotined, the idea of blaming the diamond for their misfortunes may well have begun with Pierre Cartier, who sold the Hope to Mrs. McLean.

It is even possible that the stories about the Hope diamond and Colot, Kanitovsky, Laduc, and Montharides are as recent as the 1921 book in which they appeared, *The Mystery of the Hope Diamond*. Judging from other material in this book, these four individuals could have existed and even suffered the deaths described without ever having possessed the Hope diamond. When the variety of deaths which befell them is examined, it does seem as though someone has tried very hard to make the subject interesting.

Historically, jewels have seldom been regarded as purely neutral objects. Their nature was often perceived as being good, and many jewels were used as charms to ward off evil spirits, convey special talents to the wearer, or, therapeutically, to protect one from disease.

On the other hand, the association of jewels with evil is implicit in a Persian legend about the origin of gems recounted by G. F. Kunz in his book *The Curious Lore of Precious Stones*. Satan is said to have observed how Eve was strongly attracted to the many-colored flowers in the Garden of Eden. Wishing to have as potent a weapon over the human race in his own kingdom, Satan attempted to duplicate the colors of flowers out of the earth—and so created gemstones.

The legend of bad luck associated with the Hope diamond has continued because people enjoy hearing about it, but it is founded on fiction and coincidence—consoling information considering that the diamond is now owned by the United States of America.

Notes

1. Edwin W. Streeter, *Precious Stones and Gems* (London: Chapman and Hall, 1877), page 103.
2. *Dictionary of National Biography* (London: Oxford University Press, 1921-22), vol. 9, page 1223.
3. Ibid, pages 1222-1223.
4. H. L. Gates, *The Mystery of the Hope Diamond*. From the personal narrative of Lady Francis Hope (May Yohe). (New York: International Copyright Bureau, 1921), page 93.
5. *The Law Reports of the Supreme Court of Judicature*, Sir Frederick Pollock, ed. (London: Bart, William Clower and Sons, Ltd., 1899), vol. 2, pages 688-89.
6. *The Mystery of the Hope Diamond*, page 211.
7. Wallis R. Cattelle, *The Diamond* (New York: John Lane Co., 1911), page 84; and Julius Wodiska, *A Book of Precious Stones* (New York: C. P. Putnam's Sons, The Knickerbocker Press, 1909), page 242.

8. Evalyn Walsh McLean with Boyden Sparkes, *Father Struck It Rich* (Boston: Little, Brown and Co., 1936), page 155.
9. *Time* magazine, May 5, 1947, page 26.
10. *Father Struck It Rich*, page 155.
11. Ibid., page 156.
12. Ibid., page 155.
13. Ibid., page 155-56.
14. Ibid., page 172.
15. Ibid., page 174.
16. Millie Considine and Ruth Pool, *Wills: A Dead Giveaway* (Garden City, N.Y.: Doubleday and Co., 1974), page 81.
17. Quoted by Dorothy Dignam.
18. William R. Simpson and Florence K. Simpson with Charles Samuels, *Hockshop* (New York: Random House, 1954), page 172.
19. Ibid., page 173.
20. *Father Struck It Rich*, page 143.
21. Edward Francis (Baron) Twining, *A History of the Crown Jewels of Europe* (London: B. T. Batsford, Ltd., 1960), page 248.
22. Anita de Barrera, *Gems and Jewels* (London: Richard Bentley, 1860), page 294.
23. Cattelle, *The Diamond*, page 84.
24. *The Souvenirs of Leonard*, translated by A. Teixera De Mattos (Privately printed, London, 1897), vol. 2, chapt. 5.
25. Stanley Loomis, *The Fatal Friendship* (Garden City, N.Y.: Doubleday and Co., 1972).
26. John Mawe, *A Treatise on Diamonds and Precious Stones*, 1823.
27. Nancy Mitford, *The Sun King* (New York: Harper & Row, 1966), page 84.

Chronology

FRENCH BLUE DIAMOND

1642   Purchased in India by Tavernier; weight $112\frac{1}{8}$ carats.
1668   Sold to Louis XIV.
1673   Recut to triangular shape by Sieur Pitau; new weight $67\frac{1}{8}$.
1749   Set in Order of the Golden Fleece with the Côte de Bretagne.
1792   Stolen from Garde-Meuble during French Revolution.

HOPE DIAMOND

1812   In possession of London diamond dealer Daniel Eliason.
1830   Sold by Eliason to Henry Philip Hope.
1839   Acquired by Hope's nephew, Henry Thomas Hope.
1887   Life interest inherited by Lord Francis Hope.
1901   Sold to Joseph Frankel's Sons, New York jewelers.
1908   Sold to one M. Habib in Paris.
1909   Sold to M. Aucoc of France (possibly in partnership with M. Rosenau).
1909/10   Purchased by Cartier's, French jewelers.
1911   Sold to Evalyn Walsh McLean.
1949   Sold to Harry Winston.
1958   Given to the Smithsonian Institution.

Hope Diamond Data

Size: Depth 12.05 mm
  Length 25.6 mm
  Width 21.9 mm
  Table 11.8 x 14.5 mm
  Height above Girdle 2.7 mm
  Depth below Girdle 11.3 mm

Cut: Mixed cut, producing a nonsymmetrical gem with 58 facets, plus 2 extra facets between the girdle and the top of the main pavilion facets. There are also additional facets on the girdle.

Color: Dark blue, often described as "steel blue."

Clarity: Apparently flawless.

Weight: 45.52 carats.

Other characteristics:

  Strong anomalous birefringence between crossed polaroids, indicating internal stress. Nonflorescent under ultraviolet light.

  Following exposure to ultraviolet light of less than 3,500 angstrom units, the Hope diamond phosphoresces red. All other blue diamonds of this type (IIb) phosphoresce light blue.

A diamond is evaluated by considering its cut, color, clarity (presence or absence of flaws), and carat weight.

The Hope diamond is a cushion-shaped brilliant of slightly irregular proportions. Its cut is somewhat shallow, which makes it seem large for its weight, but this also makes it fail to achieve maximum brilliance.

The blue color of the Hope qualifies it as a "fancy" diamond. The jewelry trade classifies as fancy those rare diamonds that occur in attractive shades of yellow, green, blue, or red.

Examination of the mounted Hope reveals no flaws. The diamond could not be termed flawless on this basis, however, as it is possible for the mounting to conceal small imperfections. On November 13, 1975, the Hope was removed from its mounting, probably for the first time in 65 years, and observations confirmed those of Françillon when he examined the unset diamond in 1812 and described it as "all perfection without specks or flaws."

Almost the same carat weight has been ascribed to the Hope diamond from 1812 to the present, which seems unreasonable because the weight of a carat varied from

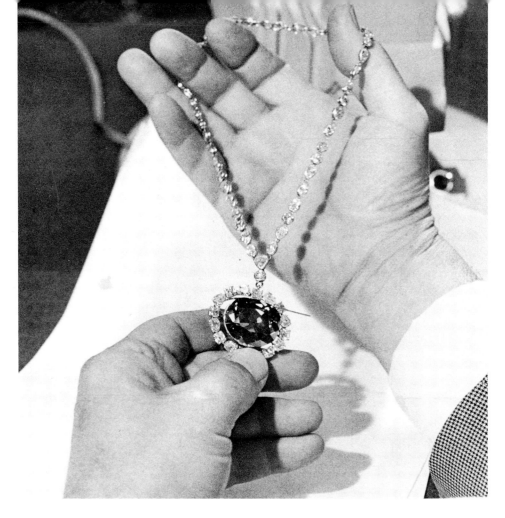

The mounting of the Hope diamond was recently modified so that the gem can be more easily removed for study. This photograph was taken as the work was in progress, as evidenced by the wire visible to the right of the diamond. The Hope is being held by Robert Limon, C.G., A.G.S., the jeweler who altered the mounting.

country to country until, by 1913, most of the major nations dealing in diamonds (with the exception of South Africa, which waited until 1923) had adopted a standardized metric carat of 200 milligrams. The 1839 catalog of Henry Philip Hope's jewel collection listed the weight of 177 grains or 44¼ carats. A spokesman for Harry Winston, Inc., said that the diamond had not been removed from its mounting in the years that Winston owned it. The weight given for the Hope on the Cartier invoice to the McLeans was 44.50 carats. Assuming that Cartier weighed the diamond in 1910 or 1911 when it was reset, the old French carat of approximately 205 milligrams would have been used. Converted into standardized carats, this produces a figure of 45.61 carats. The reasoning was borne out in November 1975 when the unmounted Hope was found to weigh 45.52 modern metric carats. At the same time, the Hope was also accurately measured (dimensions given in preceding chart).

Herbert Tillander, jeweler, gemologist, and author, of Helsinki, Finland, has researched the history of the Hope diamond with special attention to its cut and weight. The result of his research was presented in a paper delivered at the fifteenth International Gemmological Conference held in Washington, D.C., in October 1975. He came to some interesting conclusions. As part of his study, Tillander created quartz models of the Tavernier blue, the French blue, and the Hope diamond. These led him to reject the presumption, endorsed by Streeter, that one or more small diamonds may have resulted from the cutting of the French blue. He also believes it likely that the girdle of the Hope was faceted when it was in Cartier's possession.

Selected Bibliography

Bapst, Germain. *Histoire des Joyaux de la Couronne*. Paris: Librairie Hachette et Cie, 1889.

Buist, Marten G. *At Spes Non Fracta, Hope & Co. 1770-1815*. Amsterdam: Bank Mees & Hope N.V., 1974.

Carlyle, Thomas. *The French Revolution*. Modern Library edition, New York.

Gates, H. L. *The Mystery of the Hope Diamond*. New York: International Copyright Bureau, 1921.

McLean, Evalyn Walsh, with Boyden Sparkes. *Father Struck it Rich*. Boston: Little, Brown and Co., 1936.

Mitford, Nancy. *The Sun King*. New York: Harper & Row, 1966.

Streeter, Edwin W. *Precious Stones and Gems*. London: Chapman and Hall, 1877.

——. *The Great Diamonds of the World*. London: George Bell and Sons, 1882.

Tavernier, Jean Baptiste. *Travels in India*. Translated by V. Ball. Vols I and II, Macmillan & Co., 1889.

Twining, Edward Francis (Baron Twining). *A History of the Crown Jewels of Europe*. London: Bt. Batsford, 1960.

Few people have seen the Hope diamond out of its mounting. It is shown here side by side with its chain and setting as it appeared on November 13, 1975, when the gem was removed to be weighed. Previous weights for the Hope, recorded when the metric weight of the carat varied from country to country, ranged from 44 to 44½ carats. Its weight in modern carats of 200 milligrams is 45.52 carats.